Action Art

Using Color

Isabel Thomas

Heinemann Library
Chicago, Illinois

Customer Service 888-454-2279

Visit our website at www.heinemannlibrary.com

Printed and bound in China by South China Printing Company Limited
Photo research by Mica Brancic

09 08 07 06 05
10 9 8 7 6 5 4 3 2 1

Library of Congress Cataloging-in-Publication Data
Thomas, Isabel, 1980-
    Action art : using color / Isabel Thomas.
        p. cm. -- (Action art)
    Includes bibliographical references and index.
    ISBN 1-4034-6920-2 (library binding-hardcover) -- ISBN 1-4034-6926-1 (pbk.)
    1. Color in art--Juvenile literature. I. Title. II. Series.
    N7432.7.T48 2005
    701'.85--dc22
                                                                2005001577

Acknowledgments
The author and publishers are grateful to the following for permission to reproduce
copyright material: Alamy p. **5**; Corbis pp. **4**, **14**; Harcourt Education p. **10**
(Trevor Clifford) pp. **6**, **7**, **8**, **9**, **11**, **12**, **13**, **15**, **16**, **17**, **18**, **19**, **20**, **21**, **22**, **23**, **24**
(Tudor Photography)

Cover photograph of hand painting reproduced with permission of Corbis.

Every effort has been made to contact copyright holders of any material reproduced in
this book. Any omissions will be rectified in subsequent printings if notice is given to
the publisher.

Many thanks to the teachers, library media specialists, reading instructors, and educational
consultants who have helped develop the Read and Learn/Lee y aprende brand.

Some words are shown in bold, **like this.** You can
find them in the picture glossary on page 23.

Contents

What Is Art?

Art is something you make when you are being **creative**.

People like to look at art.

A person who makes art is called an artist.

You can be an artist, too!

What Kinds of Art Are There?

There are many different kinds of art.

You can draw and paint pictures.

sculpture

Try making sculptures and collage, too.

You can use color in all your art.

What Are Primary Colors?

Red, yellow, and blue are called primary colors.

We mix them together to make other colors.

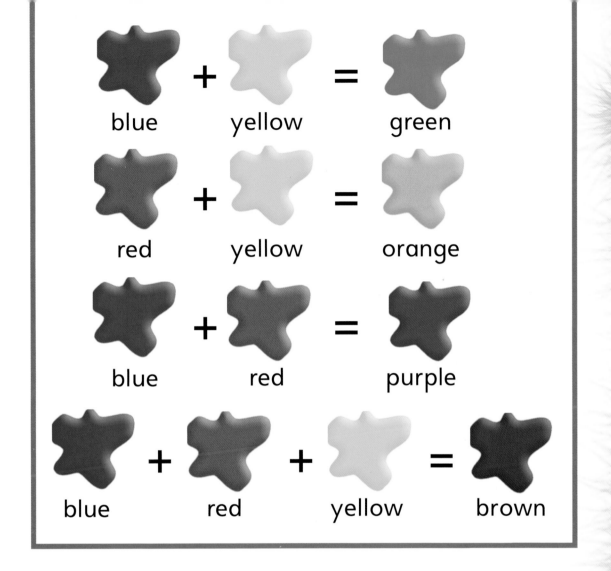

blue + yellow = green

red + yellow = orange

blue + red = purple

blue + red + yellow = brown

Try mixing paints to make these new colors.

You can use a brush or your fingers!

How Can I Make Colors Lighter or Darker?

There are light and dark **shades** of every color.

Look at the different shades of blue in this picture.

black

blue

white

Make a color darker by adding black paint.

Add white paint to make a color lighter.

What Can I Use for Coloring?

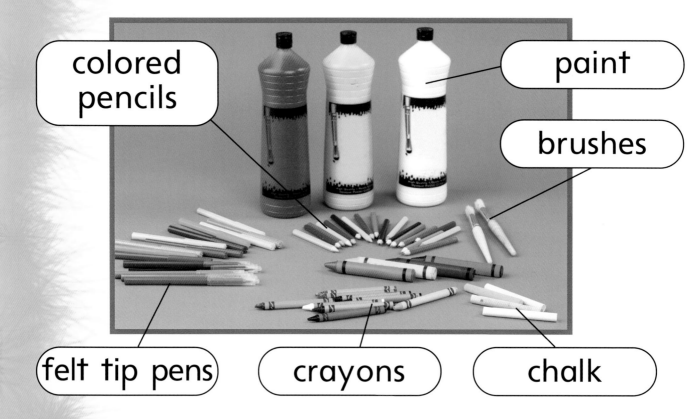

colored pencils

paint

brushes

felt tip pens

crayons

chalk

Look at all the **tools** that you can use for coloring.

You can use colorful paper and objects to make art, too.

You can make a colorful collage.

How Can I Use Color?

You can use color to make art look interesting.

Use paints to color your sculptures.

Color in your drawings carefully.

Try to keep the color inside
the lines.

How Can I Make a Pattern?

You can use lots of colors to make a **pattern**.

Try using patterns to **decorate** things.

Potato printing is a fun way to make patterns.

Print a border for your art.

How Do Colors Make Me Feel?

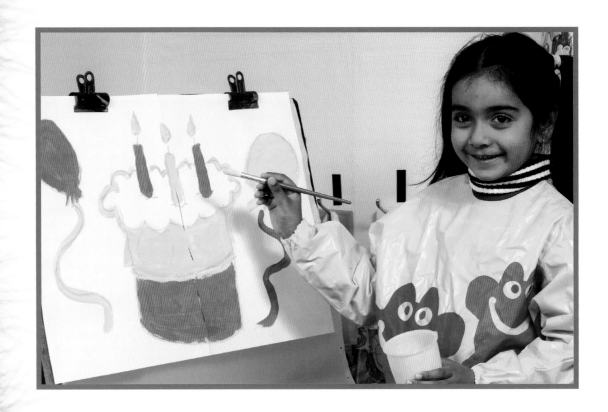

Colors can make us feel different things.

Bright colors make you feel happy.

What colors would you use to paint a bright and sunny day?

Let's Use Color!

Let's use color to make a fish!

1. Use a wax crayon to draw the shape of a big fish.

2. Fill in the shape using lots of different colored crayons. You can draw green seaweed, too.

20

3. Now paint over your drawing with watery blue paint.

4. You have made a picture of a fish in the sea!

Quiz

Can you remember which colors
you need to add to make these colors?

green = blue + ?

brown = yellow + red + ?

orange = yellow + ?

purple = red + ?

Look for the answers on page 24.

Picture Glossary

creative, page 4
making something using your own ideas
and how you feel inside

decorate, page 16
add colors and patterns to make
something look nice

pattern, page 16
the same shapes and colors used over and
over again

primary colors, page 8
red, blue, and yellow are called
primary colors

shade, page 10
different kind of one color. Light blue
and dark blue are different shades of blue.

tool, page 12
thing you use for coloring in, such as
colored pencils and crayons

Note to Parents and Teachers

Reading for information is an important part of a child's literacy development. Learning begins with a question about something. Help children think of themselves as investigators and researchers by encouraging their questions about the world around them. Each chapter in this book begins with a question. Read the question together. Look at the pictures. Talk about what you think the answer might be. Then read the text to find out if your predictions were correct. Think of other questions you could ask about the topic, and discuss where you might find the answers. Assist children in using the picture glossary and the index to practice new vocabulary and research skills.

Index

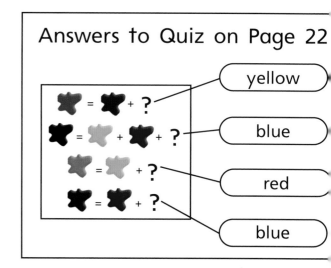

Answers to Quiz on Page 22

yellow

blue

red

blue